I0410949

1

Table of Contents

I. Development Context, Challenges and Opportunities

Overview - Moldova is a landlocked country in Europe's East located on the border of the European Union (EU) between Ukraine and Romania. With an area of 33,851 square kilometers (13,069 sq. mi.), Moldova is slightly larger than Belgium. The population is approximately 3.6 million and approximately 75% of the population is ethnic Romanians, with the balance made up of ethnic Russians and Ukrainians and smaller numbers of Gagauz (Turkic-speaking Moldovans) and Roma.

Historical Context - The area comprising modern-day Moldova was first consolidated within a larger independent state in the mid-1400s, extending from the Carpathian mountains (modern-day Romania) in the west to the Nistru river in the east. Through the 1700s the area, now a tributary of the Ottoman Empire, was contested by Ottoman, Russian and Austro-Hungarian armies, leading to the annexation by Russia in 1812 of the eastern half of the territory, located on the Black Sea between the Prut and Nistru rivers. This area, known as Bessarabia, remained a part of the Russian empire until 1917 when the Moldovan Democratic Republic declared its independence and voted to unite with Romania.

During the inter-war period Russia rejected Bessarabian unification with Romania and established a government in exile, along with a militarized and industrialized buffer zone across the Nistru river, as a platform for re-annexation. Bessarabia changed hands between Russian and combined Romanian-German armies from 1940-1944, during which time the country suffered from mass executions and deportations of Jewish and Roma populations to Nazi concentration camps. Following victory in World War II, the Soviet Union incorporated the territory, minus Black Sea coastal areas and Romanian-speaking Northern Bukovina, and including the Transnistrian buffer zone, into the Moldovan Soviet Socialist Republic (MSSR). Along with changing the historical borders, the Soviet Union also encouraged the settlement of Russians and Ukrainians in the MSSR (particularly urban areas), as well as executing or deporting tens of thousands of ethnic Romanians.

Under the Soviet Union, the MSSR continued as a major center of agricultural production and received high levels of investment in infrastructure and mechanization from the central budget. There was also significant investment in heavy industry concentrated largely in Transnistria. At the same time, the Soviet government attempted to foster the concept of a distinct Moldovan national identity and language. Under Glasnost and especially after the fall of the Berlin Wall, there were increasing expressions of support for the Romanian language and for independence. As the break-up of the Soviet Union accelerated after the abortive 1991 coup, Moldova declared independence. The new Republic of Moldova re-instituted the use of the Latin alphabet (rather than Cyrillic) for the Romanian language and adopted a flag based on the Romanian tricolor flag and, for a time, the Romanian national anthem. Fearing another reunification between Romania and Moldova, elements within the Transnistrian region - with Russian military assistance - launched a separatist movement in 1992. The short conflict led to a cease-fire policed by Russian forces and a de-facto separation of Transnistria within Moldova which exists through the present.

Political Situation - Moldova is a parliamentary republic with a Prime Minister serving as the head of government and a President as the head of state. After ten years of independence, Moldova was the first former Soviet state in which the voters returned Communists to power, with the Party of Communists of the Republic of Moldova (PCRM) in power from 2001 to 2009. A three party alliance of the Liberal Democratic Party (PLDM), the Democratic Party (PD), and the Liberal Party (PL) formed the Alliance for European Integration (AIE) and took the parliamentary majority from the PCRM in 2009 after widespread protests, based on accusations of electoral fraud, led to repeat elections. The President is elected by a super majority (3/5) vote of the Parliament. The AIE did not achieve a super majority in the parliament in the 2009 elections, resulting in extended political deadlock with the Parliament unable to elect a President. Another round of Parliamentary elections in 2010 returned the AIE to power, but still without a sufficient super majority to elect a President. Finally, in March 2012, a compromise candidate for President was proposed who attracted AIE support as well as a small group of PCRM Members of Parliament (MP) who broke ranks, resolving the three-year deadlock which had limited the AIE's ability to make progress on its reform objectives. There were always tensions within the alliance that would sometimes surface publicly, but in early 2013 these tensions intensified, resulting in a no confidence vote that removed Prime Minister Vlad Filat from office. With none of the non-Communist parties desiring early elections, a compromise was hammered out at the end of May 2013 and a new majority coalition was formed. Moldova continues to search for a way to resolve the Transnistria conflict. Settlement talks have occurred only sporadically since 2006 via the "5+2" group, composed of Moldova, Transnistria, Ukraine, Russia, and the Organization for Security and Co-operation in Europe (OSCE), with the EU and the U.S. as observers. In the December 2011 Transnistrian elections, voters rejected the long-term incumbent "President" in favor of a new leader. After a five-year hiatus, official 5+2 settlement negotiations have resumed, but progress has been slow. Ukraine assumed the Chairmanship of the OSCE and the first 5+2 meeting of 2013 took place in February in Lviv, Ukraine.

Aligned with the Government of the Republic of Moldova's (GOM) aspirations, the overarching goal of the United States is to help Moldova become a fully democratic, economically prosperous state, firmly anchored to Europe, secure within its internationally recognized borders and with an effective and accountable government. The United States, alongside the EU and other international partners, is assisting Moldova to consolidate democratic institutions, rebuild a struggling economy, improve the business environment, expand the rule of law and resolve the conflict in Transnistria.

> GOM's Moldova 2020 - National Development Strategy
> 1. Education: Relevant for a career
> 2. Roads: In Good Condition, Anywhere
> 3. Finance: Affordable and Cheap
> 4. Business: With Clear Rules of the Game
> 5. Energy: Delivered Safely, Used Efficiently
> 6. Justice: Responsible and Incorruptible
> 7. Pension System: Equitable and Sustainable

In spite of ongoing reforms, Moldova remains the poorest country in Europe with a per capita Gross National Income of $3,670 (in purchasing power parity), which is only better than Uzbekistan, Kyrgyzstan, and Tajikistan in the Europe and Eurasia region (2011 World Bank, World Development Indicators). While many challenges persist, the United States has an opportunity to leverage relatively small investments to achieve great impact by helping the Pro-European government demonstrate to its people the improved living standards that stem from democratic and economic reforms.

Challenges - The country faces many daunting challenges, primary among which are the following:

Ineffective and Corrupt Judiciary - The 2012 United States Agency for International Development (USAID) Monitoring Country Progress (MCP) analysis[1] based on the Freedom House - Nations in Transit report indicates no improvement in Rule of Law from 2002 (see chart below for democratic reform trends from 1996-2011). Public confidence in the judiciary is undermined by: 1) Excessive dependency on the executive branch; 2) Courts with huge backlogs of cases; 3) A shortage of qualified human resources; 4) Often unenforceable court decisions; 5) Low citizen expectations and knowledge of the judicial system and their rights; and 6) High judicial susceptibility to corruption. While, the GOM has made some positive steps towards reform, including dissolving the economic courts and the Parliament's passage of the Judicial Sector Reform Strategy, the sector remains one of the weakest lynchpins to development. While USAID is not the only donor recognizing this challenge, it is currently the only donor providing direct technical assistance to address the challenge. Technical assistance is vital in enabling the GOM to access budget support from the EU.

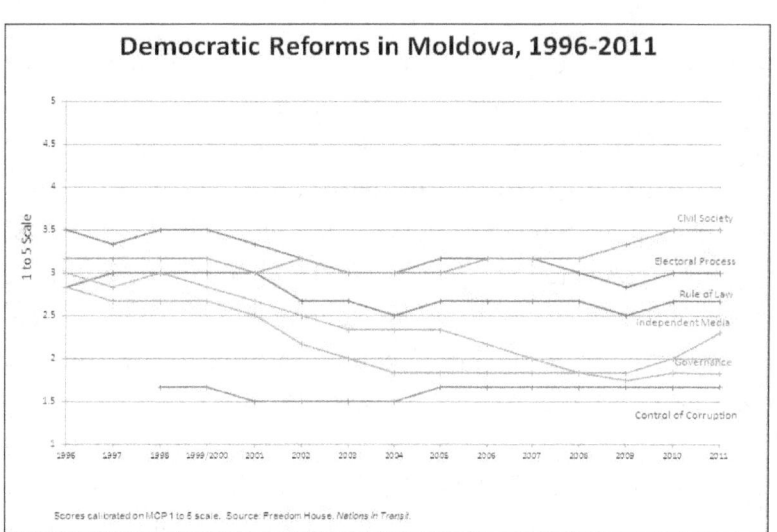

Endemic Corruption - The MCP indicates no improvement in corruption since 1998. In the 2011 Transparency International Corruption Perception Index, Moldova is tied for 112 out of 183 countries, with peers such as Egypt and Vietnam. Corruption remains a systemic problem that is deeply embedded in Moldova's public institutions. While anti-corruption legislation exists on the books and a new anti-corruption strategy was adopted, implementation remains weak and enforcement is inconsistent.

Weak Government Capacity - The MCP indicates a marked decline in Democratic Governance since 1998. Nevertheless, democratization in Moldova is more advanced than the Eastern Europe and Eurasia norm. In particular, over-centralized control of resources and political power, along with inadequate

---

[1] Annex 3 provides the MCP Gap Analysis highlights

local government capacity, have been long-term issues in Moldova. A new strategy for decentralization was developed in 2011, but actual implementation of administrative changes has been slow. At the national level there remains extremely low capacity in government, due in part to an inability to recruit or retain civil servants because of non-competitive wages, to implement government decisions and priorities despite ongoing reforms in law and regulation. This challenge is currently being addressed at the national level by the EU. USAID is working in this sector at the local level throughout the country, in coordination with the EU in 2 of the 32 Raions of rural Moldova.

Non-Communist Parties in Conflict with Each Other – At the time of publication, the non-Communist parties represented in parliament consist of PLDM, PL, and PD. PL recently broke into two factions, with its leader moving into the opposition and a majority of its MPs joining the new Pro-European Coalition. Although they share a broadly pro-EU orientation, the Pro-European Coalition parties represent a broad range of political positions ranging from socialists who were former Communists, centrists who support free-markets and reforms, and conservatives who are anti-Communists and pro-Romania. Some of the non-Communist MPs are former PCRM members who have either joined the Socialist party or who are independent.

Excessive Migration - Migration is a cross-cutting phenomenon that affects all layers of the population. The higher wages in other European labor markets continue to lure migrants including through illegal means. Migration not only causes brain drain, but has caused other negative results such as human trafficking and neglect of the children and elderly who are left behind. According to the International Organization for Migration (IOM) 2012 Migration Profile Report, the number of Moldovans living overseas is estimated between 100,000 and 300,000. This accounts for the rough estimate of one quarter of the working-age Moldovan population being outside the country. As this migration is driven predominantly by economic conditions in Moldova, the only way to reduce it is to improve economic opportunity in Moldova.

Deficient Workforce Skills - The GOM's primary development strategy document, Moldova 2020[2], stresses the importance of developing Moldova's human capital. The degradation of the education system in the past 20 years and the migration of large numbers of specialists have caused a reduction in labor skills. According to the 2010 European Bank for Reconstruction and Development (EBRD) Transition Report, work skills are the most serious constraint to business in Moldova. Causes include a weak and corrupt educational system, a significant shortage of skilled workers in key industries caused by migration, rigidities in the labor market, and a high reservation wage based on remittances. The World Bank and the EU are the predominant donors in assisting the formal education sector. USAID will focus on the public-private nexus for improving workforce skills in demand by the economy.

Lack of Economic Diversity and Competitiveness - According to the World Bank - 2012 Country Program Snapshot, agriculture has produced 12 percent of Gross Domestic Product (GDP) and employed 28 percent of the labor force with agro-food exports constituting 45-50 percent of total

---

[2] http://www.gov.md/public/files/Moldova_2020_ENG.pdf

exports. The 2012 World Economic Forum (WEF) Global Competitiveness Report[3] shows Moldova as a country with a very small and inefficient market for goods, and firms that are characterized by low levels of technological readiness, business sophistication, and innovation.

Energy Dependency and Inefficiency - EBRD and the International Monetary Fund (IMF) have noted recent progress in energy sector reforms, but Moldova's energy sector remains highly insecure by at least two broad World Bank – World Development Indicators of energy security: dependency (96% of energy used is imported), and efficiency (3.8 USD GDP per unit of energy use). These measures collectively show that Moldova has one of the most energy inefficient and energy dependent economies worldwide. Separately, the 2012 United Nations (UN) Partnership Framework[4] states that 15-25% of energy is lost due to transmission and distribution inefficiencies. The most significant assistance for Moldova in this area is the planned gas pipeline from Romania. This combined with the changing market for gas in Europe could provide Moldova other sources of energy. EBRD is the major donor in the area of energy efficiency, supplemented by other donors such as the German International Development Cooperation Agency (GIZ) and USAID, who through concentrating on improving local government capacity facilitate the conversion to or construction of more energy efficient facilities.

Poor Infrastructure - The 2012 WEF Global Competitiveness Report ranks the country's overall infrastructure in the lower 20% due to the lack of needed investment or budget. Poor road and irrigation quality, along with other limitations in physical infrastructure, remain impediments to investment and trade. The European Union and Millennium Challenge Corporation (MCC) are significant donors in these areas. Through these efforts, Moldovan roads conditions are making significant progress. The irrigation systems being financed by MCC will restore a significant capacity in Moldova for agriculture, which USAID will seek to further leverage in its economic growth programs. The MCC Compact[5] is at the half way point in implementation and remains on track to reach a successful conclusion. If a second Compact is negotiated during the timeframe of this Country Development Cooperation Strategy (CDCS), USAID will seek opportunities for innovative collaboration such as the one in the first Compact.

Limited Access to Finance - Despite well-capitalized, liquid, and generally sound banks, the small size of the financial sector and the limited range of available financial products and services continue to constrain economic growth in the private sector. At the same time, most Moldovans do not have confidence in the banking system, with large numbers of people preferring to keep savings in cash or other assets. EBRD has prioritized financing for private and public infrastructure projects, financial institutions and support to local small and medium enterprises. In the area of energy efficiency, EBRD is extending credit lines to local banks for lending to corporate and residential borrowers that undertake energy efficiency projects and sustainable energy investments. To augment EBRD's financing and complement local government energy efficiency initiatives, USAID will explore a co-guarantee loan

---

[3] http://www.weforum.org/reports/global-competitiveness-report-2011-2012
[4] http://www.un.md/key_doc_pub/
[5] http://www.mcc.gov/pages/countries/overview/moldova

facility with the Swedish International Development Cooperation agency (SIDA) that focuses on unaddressed borrower groups, particularly in rural areas.

Transnistria Frozen Conflict - While full-scale military conflict appears unlikely to re-emerge, the break-away region persists as a challenge to a unified and developed Moldova. Despite encouraging progress, the negotiations process will require patience and persistence in dealing with the most contentious issues on Transnistria's status and Russia's military presence. Continued separation complicates overland commercial and private transportation to Ukraine, adds complexity to customs issues, and provides additional venues for corruption, thus impeding the development of a healthy market economy. While movement is relatively easy between both banks of the Nistru, there is the risk that those without commercial, family, or personal ties on the other side of the river will increasingly feel estranged from their fellow Moldovans, fostering the kind of mistrust and misunderstanding that can further hinder the resolution of this conflict.

Opportunities - Achieving greater integration with Europe remains Moldova's highest-level foreign policy objective. It also remains a significant part of most parties' platforms and remains popular among voters. While Europe is key to Moldova's future, economic ties with both the East and the West are seen as a real advantage. In the face of the Eurozone crisis, the IMF still projects positive GDP growth in Moldova because of the resilient conditions of trading partners in the Commonwealth of Independent States (CIS). Improving the business-enabling environment and expanding market linkages, both with the East and West, will support trade and investment diversification, mitigate the contagion effect of one region's economic woes, and help to expand the benefits of reforms.

Of the seven MCP measurements on democratic reforms, civil society is the most advanced in Moldova, and is the only aspect that has advanced on balance since 1996. However, while some civil society organizations (CSOs) continue to play a key role in political life and are active in advancing reform efforts, civil society as a whole still remains weak overall. Per the UN, while CSOs are active, diverse, and dynamic at the national level, there is a need for further expansion of democratic space and participation at the local levels. Moreover, CSOs still struggle to sustain themselves financially with local resources and are heavily dependent on foreign donors. Individual CSOs, and the sector as whole, require continued donor support to buttress financial viability, subject expertise, and constituent engagement with the aim of consolidating achievements to date and preventing backsliding. The USAID Forward goal to promote local capacity development further reinforces the rationale for continued donor support in these areas. Civil society is imperative to Moldova's transition and securing democratic institutions. CSOs can play a vital role in Moldova by supplying independent research, advocating for reform, keeping watch over governmental inefficiency, dereliction, and abuse, and providing important social services.

As shown in the MCP, Moldova's independent media has made notable gains in 2010 and 2011, after considerable backsliding in earlier years. With the increase in private sector investments in media and the development of a regional TV network, Moldovans now have greater access to a broader array of opinions. Concerns remain about shortcomings, particularly the degree to which media holdings are affiliated with various political parties. Nevertheless, successes with past assistance in the media sector can be leveraged to bolster citizen engagement and governmental oversight.

With the restart of formal "5+2" talks and the leadership transition in Tiraspol, prospects for resolution of the Transnistrian conflict have grown and the United States, as a formal observer to the "5+2", has activated efforts to aid confidence-building and the reconciliation process by engaging with Transnistrian officials, businesses, NGOs, media and academia. USAID can support the reintegration objective with opportunistic assistance to Transnistrian local governments, CSOs and micro, small and medium enterprises (MSMEs) to promote local development in Transnistria and to build linkages between communities on both sides of the Nistru river. Moreover, as opportunities to influence change in Transnistria arise, the Mission can incorporate activities that are consistent with USAID's Implementation Plan for the U.S. National Action Plan for Women, Peace and Security by engaging women leaders in trust-building activities.

II. Development Hypothesis

In preparation for the development of the CDCS, USAID/Moldova engaged in a process of analysis and consultation to gather information for the new five-year strategic plan. USAID/Moldova held a staff retreat in May 2012 to formally kick-off the process. At the same time, the Moldova office initiated consultations with stakeholders in the host government, the private sector, other donor agencies, the U.S. embassy in Chisinau, and within USAID's technical offices. These consultations focused on soliciting perspectives on the key development challenges facing Moldova, as well as the most likely areas where assistance could achieve the greatest impact.

To gather more detailed technical information in key areas, USAID/Moldova launched four new external and independent sector assessments, including Democracy, Human Rights, and Governance; Economic Growth; Biodiversity; and Donor Mapping of International Development Assistance activities in Moldova. The Moldova office also reviewed and reconfirmed the validity of the recently-completed (March 2011) Moldova Gender Assessment. (See Annex 4)

Upon completion of these assessments and stakeholder consultations, USAID/Moldova hosted a CDCS workshop in September 2012. The workshop facilitated a discussion process that provided guidance for developing the CDCS and led the Moldova team through detailed results framework development discussions.

In addition to this analysis, USAID/Moldova relied heavily on the accumulated experience of nearly 20 years of working in the country, both from the personal experience of its local staff, the reports of previous activities, and the comments and impressions on these activities from Moldovan government and private sector interlocutors. Moldova is a small country and this provides important advantages such as ease of access to key decision makers and a small number of stakeholders when it comes time to seek and obtain buy-in on important reforms. Together with the close coordination with other international donors, this makes it possible to have significant results even with fairly modest programs.

The result of these consultations, studies, and meetings, as well as implementation experience, is a clear goal statement supported by two mutually-reinforcing development objectives.

Goal: A Better-Governed Moldova with Improved Living Standards for its Citizens

As described in the Department of State and USAID Joint Regional Strategy (JRS) 2014-2016 for Europe and Eurasia, the overarching U.S. government goal for countries in Europe's East is to consolidate peace and stability. Noting that Moldova's democracy is the strongest in the region, the JRS states that in Moldova "we will build on our efforts to strengthen democratic governance, improve the business climate, build a growing economy, combat corruption, reform the justice sector, and leverage MCC activities... helping the Western-oriented government demonstrate to its people the improved living standards that stem from democratic and economic reforms.[6]" To provide a strategic foundation from which to develop programs to address the challenges identified in the JRS and through the consultation and assessment process, the CDCS goal is supported by two Development Objectives (DOs): 1) More Effective and Accountable Democratic Governance; and 2) Increased Broad-Based Trade and Investment.

USAID/Moldova's strategy asserts that by working to consolidate Moldova's democratic institutions and processes, the country can expedite its economic potential for the benefit of all citizens. The strategy assumes that democratic and economic gains are closely and inextricably related, and that women and men have different social and cultural roles in Moldova which shape their ability to participate in development activities. Without real economic opportunities, however, there is a risk that Moldovans - both women and men - will give up hope in the promise of democracy and European integration. At the same time, without improvements in Moldova's ability to control corruption and give citizens an active voice in government, there is little hope of increasing investor confidence and strengthening the country's private sector. The goal, importantly, is focused on achieving tangible increases in living standards for all citizens, regardless of gender, because if Moldova cannot provide an improved quality of life for its citizens, then the most talented, skilled, and educated people will continue to leave the country.

As described in the gender assessment informing this strategy (see Annex 4 for synopsis), a special emphasis on supporting full integration of women into the political domain and business community is key to reaching this development goal. The USAID gender assessment found that two of the most pressing gender issues in Moldova are the low level of female representation in political parties and elected offices and weak economic empowerment for women. There are gains that can be made toward gender equality on both fronts if development assistance is carefully targeted toward promoting greater inclusiveness.

---

[6] State Department – Bureau of European and Eurasian Affairs USAID – Europe and Eurasia Bureau Joint Regional Strategy FY 2014 through FY 2016. p. 32.

Transnistria: With the EU providing significant resources for civil society in this breakaway region, the appropriate niche for USAID is fostering the inclusion of Transnistrians in the economic life of Moldova, increasing their understanding of the opportunities and benefits of economic relations with Europe and also increasing contacts between the business people of both banks of the Nistru. This will be accomplished through implementing USAID activities wherever possible on both banks of the Nistru.

USAID assistance alone, however, will not be sufficient to achieve the development objectives presented in this strategy. The results framework incorporates the closely-coordinated, current and planned work of other U.S. agencies, including MCC and the State Department's Bureau of International Narcotics and Law Enforcement (INL), as well as of other bilateral and multilateral donors.

Development Objective 1: More Effective and Accountable Democratic Governance

The Democracy, Human Rights, and Governance (DRG) assessment which informs this strategy found that while Moldova has made great strides since independence in the area of democracy, it remains a "borderline and unconsolidated democracy." In particular, the report notes that corruption and clientelism remain prevalent, and that there is a lack of connection between citizens' needs and the government's reform agenda. In developing its argument for the most pressing areas in need of engagement in response to these problems, the report points to weaknesses in two particular areas, notably rule of law and government effectiveness, both of which relate directly to the disconnect between citizens and the state and result in the country's weak economic performance. These areas of concern emerged repeatedly throughout the consultation process. The judicial system, in particular, stands out as the fundamental area in need of improvement in Moldova, and is an area of significant and coordinated donor engagement. Institutional strengthening support to improve rule of law and government effectiveness, along with targeted support to increase citizens' involvement in the governance process, is therefore the foundation of this development objective. The development hypothesis supporting this objective is that in Moldova, if citizen demand for good governance, enforced by a fair and impartial judicial system, meets with strengthened local government capacity, then more effective and accountable democratic governance will result. USAID interventions aimed at strengthening government capacity will be focused on those critical areas where other donor support is minimal and where the GOM and other international donors are actively seeking support. So in the judicial system, technical assistance for the judiciary from USAID and for law enforcement bodies from INL are areas where coordinated U.S. assistance can best address identified needs, while within the overall area of government effectiveness, USAID support to increase local government capacity builds on previous work done and addresses needs in an area underserved by other donors. Additionally, in both these sectors (judicial and local government), citizen oversight, engagement, and participation are essential, requiring a robust civil society and competing democratic political parties that operate in a sustainable regulatory environment and have close connections with their constituencies. In this construct, institutional strengthening at the levels of local government and the judiciary ensures that both are more responsive to the citizens, and accountable to the law and to the citizens for performing their duties properly. The concept of effective governance is therefore meant to capture 1) the capacity of an independent civil service to deliver high-quality public services, 2) transparent and responsive policy formulation informed by citizen needs, and 3) the credibility of the government's sustainability and adaptiveness as social and economic pressures evolve. The intermediate results are designed to emphasize gender equality and to be mutually reinforcing such that elements of demand for and of supply of better governance are both addressed.

The experience gained through previous and current USAID programming in this area shows that progress has already been made and gives hope that further progress can be achieved. For example, although civil society is not yet considered sustainable, progress has already been achieved in the legal and regulatory environment, making it easier for civil society organizations to register, operate, and raise funds. In the judicial sector, work on fielding an Integrated Case Management System, as well as audio recording equipment, has already ensured that the system is present in each courtroom, staff have been trained in its operation, and much of the system is being regularly used. Support among mayors in Moldova for a new local government activity is enthusiastic and owes much to the previous positive experience of these mayors with previous USAID activities. Further supporting the hypothesis that USAID support can achieve results in this sector is the fact that USAID has been able to close out activities in the media and with the Central Election Commission upon attaining desired results.

Development Objective 2: Increased Investment and Trade in Targeted Sectors

As highlighted by the Economic Growth assessment supporting the CDCS process, Moldova must broaden and increase its trade and investment base as the fundamental component of a growing economy that can provide adequate opportunities for all citizens. The development objective in this area focuses on the constraints to growth and investment in Moldova's most competitive economic sectors. By working on the structural, regulatory, and policy-level challenges that are necessary to help integrate Moldova into the European economy, as well as on increasing Moldova's ability to compete regionally by targeting assistance to the country's most promising economic sectors, the strategy concentrates USAID's efforts on helping Moldova to provide economic opportunities at home that will raise incomes, create jobs, and improve living standards for both men and women. The objective includes work being supported by other donors, which is critical to achieving this goal in Moldova. The development hypothesis which supports this objective is that strengthening Moldova's foundation for economic growth through a focus on improving the business and trade enabling environment and increasing access to finance -- while at the same time helping to empower the private sector to compete more effectively domestically and regionally -- will enable Moldova to increase foreign and domestic investment and broaden its export base.

A good example of the results that have already been achieved in this sector is Moldova's improvement in the Ease of Doing Business survey. Since 2008, Moldova has improved by 20 places. Additionally, recent leadership changes in the State Tax Service shows that the Moldovan government is responsive to donor recommendations and has the political will to get reform back on track. After a very positive IMF report in the spring of 2012, reform had temporarily stalled. The improvement in the sector up to

2012 shows that progress can be made and the recent leadership change has been evaluated within the donor community as what was needed to move forward again.

III. Results Framework

USAID will support Moldova's ambitious reform process by strengthening democratic institutions and processes while at the same time helping to create an environment favorable for the increased investment and trade required for job creation and growth. This strategy will seek to increase transparency and accountability as key drivers in strengthening democracy and unlocking the country's potential for economic growth. These improvements will lead to improved living standards for all Moldovans and demonstrate to citizens the benefits of continued reforms. USAID assistance will at the same time help Moldova to become more integrated with the rest of Europe, both politically and economically. In this way, Moldova will benefit both from the immediate gains of a stronger democracy and a growing economy, both of which strengthen the country's candidacy for European Union association and eventual membership. All USAID programs will be developed and implemented taking into consideration a cross-cutting civil society development approach in order to ensure that USAID's activities engage citizens as stakeholders in the reform process and provide them with tools to fight against corruption. Activities will also ensure that women and men have equal access to opportunities for participation and that gender disparities are targeted for elimination. While graduation from U.S. assistance is beyond the timeline of this strategy, USAID will also begin to strengthen the government of Moldova's own host country systems to respond to development challenges, such that USAID assistance plays a transformative role.

Moldova Results Framework

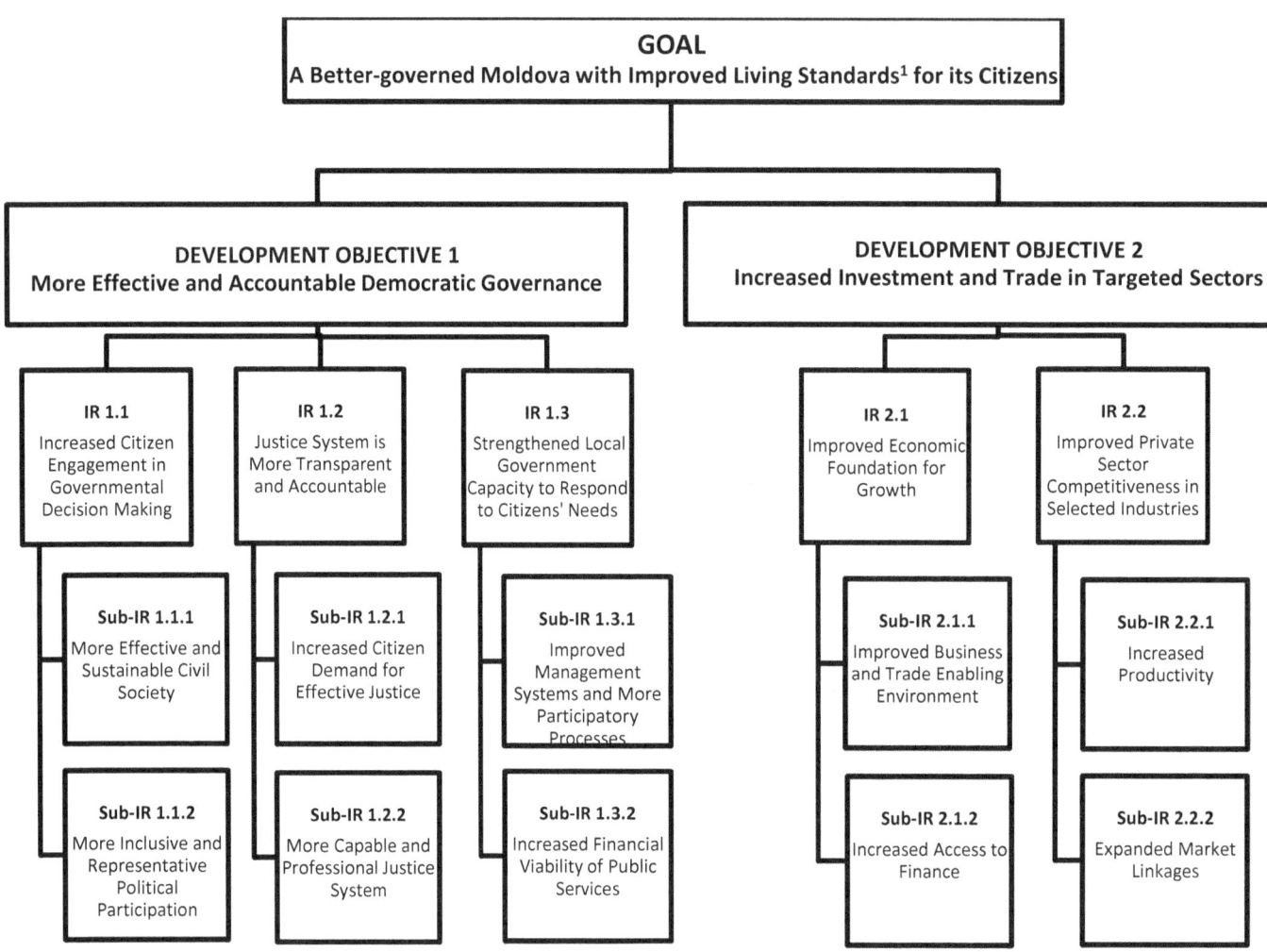

[1] GNI per capita (Purchasing Power Parity in US Dollars), as defined by the living standards dimension of UNDP's Human Development Index.

Development Objective 1: More Effective and Accountable Democratic Governance

The DRG assessment which informs this strategy found that Moldova remains a transitional democracy in need of external assistance to consolidate the reforms and improvements of recent years. At the same time, the DRG assessment notes that assistance is important in order to support other democratic reforms which have been adopted but are yet to be implemented. This Development Objective (DO) will respond to these needs to help strengthen Moldova's democratic processes and institutions. Under the activities within the objective, Moldovan citizens will become better engaged as active participants in the governance process through activities designed to strengthen the civil society sector and build institutional pathways among CSOs, government and citizens. The objective will also focus efforts on increasing the government's capacity to perform critical functions, particularly at the local government level to be more responsive and responsible to citizens. Within the U.S. government, in addition to USAID, State Department/Public Diplomacy and INL funding also support this objective. Activities funded by other donors, particularly EU technical assistance and budget support to the justice sector and for public administration, are also important components of success under the objective.

Among competing priorities, USAID will not be focusing on media during this strategy period. However, complementary media-related activities will be incorporated into DO1 to support civil society watchdog and oversight functions, such as investigative journalism.

Intermediate Result (IR) 1.1: Increased Citizen Engagement in Governmental Decision-Making
Moldova lacks a strong and effective citizen voice in governance. This weakens the quality of government decision-making and helps create an environment in which corruption can prosper. Achievement of this result will be seen when both civil society and political parties forge stronger connections with their constituents and are able to use this increased engagement to have quality and timely input into government decision making and are able to fulfill their watchdog functions and act as a restraint on corrupt actors. In a discussion of the inclusion of all segments of the population in Moldova's democracy, the DRG assessment found a "disconnect between national elites and ordinary people." The assessment went on to note that the lack of political and economic inclusion of ordinary citizens in Moldova is a key driver of migration and feeds into a vicious cycle of negative expectations and weak citizen participation. In order to bridge the gap between the state and its citizenry and to develop a more involved, participatory democracy, activities under IR 1.1 will strengthen Moldova's civil society and will focus on impediments to effective political participation facing citizens. The assessment also noted that a mature civil society is imperative to Moldova's democratic success to hold government more accountable to citizen's needs. This is why it is essential to work not just on building the capacity of civil society to engage with government but also to improve the legal and regulatory environment for civil society and the sector's managerial capacity so that civil society will be able to exercise the accountability function over the long haul and to be respected as a professional interlocutor. Moreover, the assessment noted that USAID is the only donor effort focusing on capacity building for civil society. As a result, citizens will be able to advocate more effectively to public officials and political party leaders, particularly at the local level, in order to influence the development of citizen-focused policy platforms and agendas. They also increasingly will have access to information about governance issues, such as anti-corruption and judicial reform efforts, which directly affect perceptions about Moldova's future.

<u>Sub-IR 1.1.1 More Effective and Sustainable Civil Society</u>
Despite positive steps Moldovan CSOs have taken to improve their capacity, a serious disconnect remains between CSOs areas of focus and the interests of the average Moldovan citizens. Many of the most prominent CSOs in Moldova are political think-tanks, which produce valuable studies and research, but do not lead to associated policy changes or directly respond to citizens' interests. As such, civil society in Moldova remains insufficiently representative of a broad range of constituents and does not provide an effective check on government.

One of the key recommendations of the DRG assessment for Moldova is that USAID should strengthen civil society's oversight and watchdog capacities. The report also notes that CSOs in Moldova are almost completely dependent upon donors for funding and that CSOs consequently have little control over their strategic direction. This is further exacerbated by a legal and fiscal environment that impedes the diversification of CSOs funding sources. Under this sub-IR, USAID will seek to strengthen the capacity of CSOs both to advocate independently on a broad range of issues, as well as to become more financially sustainable through broadening their resource base. USAID will also seek to build the capacity of CSOs to function as watchdogs over the government's reform progress and to gain visibility in the media in this role. This support will also empower CSOs to advocate for changes to the legal and regulatory framework needed to allow for growth, development and sustainability of the non-governmental sector.

The DRG Assessment also highlighted the necessity of strengthening "citizens' role in demanding good governance by empowering citizens through civic education, so as to help citizens understand their rights and, equally vital, their responsibilities in the democratic process, and the role of each of the various governmental and nongovernmental actors." USAID will support efforts to build a more vibrant and engaged civil society that can better serve the interests of Moldovan citizens. Activities will be designed to ensure that diverse minority and vulnerable groups receive equal consideration for assistance under this objective. Local CSO partners are expected to represent a broad range of sectors and all regions of Moldova, including the Transnistria region.

Improving the legal and regulatory environment will influence the entire sector without having to work in each segment of the sector. USAID will achieve focus and exercise selectivity through working with CSOs that focus on policy advocacy/influence and on capacity building services. To enhance the sustainability of NGOs, USAID will support CSO initiatives that allow for CSO social entrepreneurship and public contracting as revenue generation activities. This will enable the government to outsource the provision of appropriate social services to civil society providers. Not only will the implementation of such measures help to stabilize CSOs financially, but also it will also encourage CSOs to be more transparent and accountable to the local actors which support them. In alignment with the local capacity development goals of the USAID Forward agenda, the Mission will also increase direct awards to targeted local CSOs with the potential to continue playing an important role in strengthening the sector as a whole. These efforts will advance the Implementation and Procurement Reform goals of USAID Forward and position these CSOs to serve as effective civil society leaders and partners in long-term reform efforts. Moreover, USAID will endeavor to leverage assistance in this IR to complement and supplement other IRs.

Coordination with other donors shows that USAID is unique in being willing and able to work at building the capacity of the civil society sector, as opposed to just providing grants to existing CSOs. USAID's willingness to take on this challenge is particularly appreciated by other donors. Through

USAID's previous work, it is considered to have the best capacity to work in this area and it is an area that is widely recognized as being critical to success in the sector.

<u>Sub-IR 1.1.2 More Inclusive and Representative Political Participation</u>
Activities under this sub-IR were designed based on the past programmatic experiences in Moldova. While past programming was focused on enabling political competition, the new approach will engage with both the supply and demand sides of political development and participation. As such, activities will aim to improve the quality of political representation in Moldova by working directly with willing democratic political parties and with civic groups. Activities will focus on addressing the long-term developmental needs of a democratic political system by increasing parties' professional capacity at all levels and enhancing ties between political parties and citizens, with a focus at the grassroots level. Activities will promote gender equality and foster leadership of women's groups within political parties. The professional skills of party representatives will be developed to enhance their capacity to act as effective pressure points for reform and promote their active involvement in policy formulation and decision-making. These activities are intended to result in stronger linkages between political parties, civil society and governing institutions; to promote party internal democracy, transparency and accountability; and to increase the participation of citizens and emerging leaders in the political process. In this way, activities under this sub-IR are intended to result in more democratic political parties, with improved governance capacity, and more inclusive and responsive policies.

Outreach activities will help ordinary citizens to gain an understanding of the role political participation plays in a democratic society and will provide them with both the knowledge and skills to demand more responsiveness and accountability from political parties and political officials. Agents of change and pressure points from inside and outside of the parties, such as business organizations and women's groups, will be cultivated and strengthened in order to motivate parties to become more inclusive and representative democratic institutions. Political parties will be provided the impetus to encourage and develop avenues for citizen input into political parties' policies and agendas. The U.S. government will assist political parties to become more democratic and effective by working with them on institutional development, internal systems, more transparent party financing, and best practices to build transparent and accountable operations. By supporting the professional development of party leaders and staffers, USAID's work will enable them to serve their constituencies more effectively. Professional development will focus on skills necessary to design and implement more inclusive, representative and relevant policies and platforms. By building the capacity of local branches to engage with citizens and with their national party offices, this work will contribute to creating demand for representation and accountability from within party branches at the grassroots level.

In the electoral processes arena, Moldova has well-functioning electoral management systems that have received significant capacity building and technical assistance through U.S. and other donor efforts. This progress is demonstrated by free and fair elections in 2009, 2010, and 2011, and was noted by the recent DRG assessment. Experience with the United Nations Development Program (UNDP) team gained through a coordinated program in this area has confirmed USAID's analysis that UNDP will continue to be an effective and reliable partner for the Moldovan Central Election Commission. The progress already attained and the pledges from current donors to continue assistance in areas still needing improvement allow USAID to tighten its focus by ending support in the electoral processes area and shifting resources elsewhere in the sector, in particular to civil society support. Continued assistance in elections administration will be led by other donors, particularly UNDP for logistical and administrative support to hold national level elections in 2014 (or as may be announced). For upcoming national-level elections, USAID will actively participate in the donor coordination process. USAID assistance could include assistance in areas such as elections observation and voter education.

IR 1.2: Justice System is More Transparent and Accountable

Nowhere in Moldova is the need for reform more evident than in the justice sector. In reaching the conclusion that "dysfunctional rule of law is a central problem for democracy in Moldova," the DRG assessment team noted that the justice sector does not effectively constrain corruption, and is the "least legitimate branch of government." There is widespread public perception that the justice system is corrupt, ineffective, and biased toward elites. Problems are widespread across the sector. As with all Moldovan public servants, the judges, prosecutors and court personnel in Moldova are poorly paid and do not receive adequate training. The assessment noted that weak rule of law permeates Moldovan life and subverts developmental possibilities in everything from economic growth to citizen confidence. The share of Moldova's national budget spent on the justice sector is among the lowest in the region and does not provide adequate resources for effective court administration.

Judges are immune from prosecution or arrest and are not required in civil and administrative cases to record their rationale for reaching a decision. These issues are likely to be of particular relevance to women who are more frequently victims of domestic violence or trafficking. Without a culture of impartial, fair justice applying to all citizens there are few effective restrictions on corruption. Only when allegations of corruption are published in the media and create a public scandal is there pressure on the justice system to act, and this type of pressure only emerges in the most egregious of cases. In this environment, challenges to media freedom through questionable court decisions are particularly troubling because of their discouraging effect on the press' ability to investigate and report on corruption.

For these reasons, assistance will be targeted to increase the transparency and professionalism of the judiciary to improve both the accountability and independence of judges. According to Nations in Transit 2013[7], political influence in the justice system persists, and reforms should continue to work toward ensuring greater judicial independence from political pressures. Institutional structures should ensure that decisions are guided by law, precedent and procedure, and that judges can be held to account - through transparent and official means - for questionable decisions. Accountability in this sense means that appropriate mechanisms for verification, appeal and judicial censure are in place. Answerability and enforcement are important dimensions of the concept of accountability.

---

[7] http://www.freedomhouse.org/report/nations-transit/nations-transit-2013

The justice sector is a focus of donor attention and the United States is working closely alongside other key donors in the Moldovan justice sector coordination council, particularly the EU, to help implement the Government of Moldova's justice sector reform strategy. Within the U.S. government, both INL and USAID are focusing efforts on justice sector reform, with State/INL focused on criminal law, and USAID assistance focused on civil law and court administration. As criminal justice is a necessary component of the integrated country strategy, INL will be the U.S. lead for this sector.

Progress in the justice sector can only be attained through a multi-faceted approach that includes the involvement of Moldovans both individually and especially through civil society. Without a sustainable civil society, the voice of Moldovans will be diminished and the chances of progress reduced. The justice sector has a particular status because it is the one assistance area where there are significant resources brought to bear from not only USAID but also INL. Additionally, while the justice sector is important, progress within the sector would not be sufficient to address the higher level objective of more effective and accountable democratic governance. Focusing exclusively on this sector would likely render efforts unsustainable, as citizens would lack the tools for common action through civil society and political parties and would lack opportunities for involvement in their local communities.

Sub-IR 1.2.1 Increased Citizen Demand for Effective Justice

As noted above, Moldovans widely perceive the justice system to be ineffective and unfair. While there is certainly cause for this perception, ordinary citizens also lack access to information about justice sector reforms. Before citizens can become constructively engaged in dialogue about the justice sector, they must be informed on both accounts - the actual workings of justice sector processes and the government's progress in implementing reforms. Sustainability of the justice sector reform requires engaged CSOs, investigative media and active citizen monitoring in order to oversee the reform efforts, including direct support for implementation of the judicial reform strategy. This sub-IR will address these needs through work with citizens' groups including support to CSOs involved in monitoring and public reporting on justice sector reform implementation. In support of USAID Forward local capacity development goals, the Mission will focus on building the capacity of these CSOs with the aim of transitioning some subgrantees to become direct USAID partners in sustaining advocacy efforts for justice reform. In particular, USAID will work with women's NGOs to monitor courts and the justice system on issues of special importance to women. USAID will also provide capacity building assistance to media organizations and journalists in order to promote high-quality reporting on justice sector issues.

In addition, USAID will work with the courts to help them make information available to citizens about the various tools, such as court automation, that aim to increase the accountability of the judiciary. Activities will include development and deployment of new technologies for case management, for example the integrated case management system, audio recording and archiving systems for the courtrooms and websites for ease of access to information for citizens and legal professionals. This assistance to courts will also improve litigants' understanding of how to make the best use of these reforms and innovations. Through these efforts, this sub-IR will increase the quantity and quality of public knowledge about the justice sector, leading to a cycle of better informed citizens more effectively engaging with government to advocate for continuing progress in implementing reforms.

<u>Sub-IR 1.2.2 More Capable and Professional Justice System</u>
In order to carry out their mandate to interpret and apply Moldovan laws to resolve disputes fairly, as well as to protect ordinary citizens from abuses of corruption, the personnel in the justice system - including judges but also other court personnel - must be adequately trained, equipped, and provided with appropriate resources. Through this sub-IR, USAID will work directly with Moldovan courts in order to strengthen the court administration processes and systems, such as case management, budgeting and human resources. At the same time, assistance will focus on the national-level judicial institutions that are responsible for selection, training, budgeting, and assignment of judicial personnel to help them to be more effective in performing their duties. This support will enable judicial personnel to comply with mandates for reform of court processes, particularly those that respond to requirements for court processes to be open and transparent. Curriculum to train judges and other justice sector personnel will incorporate gender equality, women's rights, and relevant gender-related legislation. In addition, USAID will work to strengthen budgeting and resource management in courts, allowing for actual resource requirements to be compiled at the national level in order to inform resource decisions for courts including personnel, equipment, facilities and administrative costs. Through these activities, the courts and the judicial institutions that support them will become more efficient and effective in implementing reforms and in responding to citizen demands for justice.

Recognizing that building public trust in the rule of law also requires complementary efforts with law enforcement institutions, the strategy incorporates necessary support led by INL. Moldova's law enforcement is severely strained by chronic underfunding, poor training and lax ethics. INL assistance will support improved law enforcement and criminal justice capacity, and also strengthen Moldova's efforts to eliminate human trafficking. Collectively, these activities under IR 1.2 will help to combat corruption, which remains a core concern for sustaining progress in all other areas of assistance.

IR 1.3: Strengthened Local Government Capacity to Respond to Citizens' Needs
As citizens become more informed and effective in advocating for their interests, the government of Moldova must also improve their institutional capacity to respond to citizens' needs. With national political institutions and actors so disconnected from ordinary citizens, local government is the structure closest to the people and often the most trusted. It is at this level that citizens are best able to both participate in government policy making and also see the results of their engagement. Strengthened local government capacity will show itself in improved service delivery, which will be the most tangible evidence of achieving this result. One of the most fundamental reform processes that the government is implementing in this regard in Moldova is fiscal and administrative decentralization. Implementation of the government's National Strategy for Decentralization (NSD)[8] requires strong management and administrative capacity at the local government level in order to respond to the real and everyday needs of citizens and spur community development and economic opportunities.

---

[8] http://www.descentralizare.gov.md/index.php?l=en

Moreover, women continue to be underrepresented in local government with women accounting for 17.5% of all the mayors in Moldova, but representing around 50% of the population. These considerations are particularly important as it is this level of government that is closest to citizens and through which citizens can become involved on issues of most immediate concern. USAID assistance will therefore promote gender equality of men and women in the decision making process. Simultaneously, local government support also includes a strong citizen engagement component to foster citizen demand for effective services, bring priorities in conjunction with local needs and empower local ownership of the development and sustainability of community initiatives.

It is critical that national-level institutions in Moldova also become more effective in public administration and public financial management, including reform and restructuring of the civil service system. While this effort is largely beyond USAID's capacity, other donors, particularly the EU and the World Bank, are working in at this level. USAID will complement these national level efforts largely by working at the local level, particularly at the district capital level (the highest level of local government), where there is much less donor activity. However, USAID will also strengthen national-level procurement and financial management processes that affect the work of local and regional government institutions through the implementation of Government-to-Government (G2G) assistance activities.

Sub-IR 1.3.1 Improved Management Systems and More Participatory Processes
Through this sub-IR, USAID will work with government authorities at the local level to improve their capacity to plan for, procure and deliver basic public services, including water and sanitation, transportation, waste management, and efficient energy supply. Assistance will focus on developing the administrative and planning capacity of governments that are charged with increased responsibility for service delivery under the NSD. Core functions such as strategic planning, budgeting, and financial management will be emphasized in order to build this capacity. By working with national-level host country procurement systems to implement G2G assistance in coordination with these local government strengthening efforts, this sub-IR will develop Moldovan governmental capacity to become more effective in directing national resources through transparent and accountable procurement systems to address local development priorities, thus supporting USAID Forward - Implementation and Procurement Reform goals.

As a part of the efforts to strengthen local governments' management systems and processes, USAID will build increased human capacity within local government offices in order to ensure that civil servants have the skills to manage these new administrative tools. USAID will focus assistance on the skills that local government authorities need in order to deliver basic public services more efficiently. As a key component of this capacity building, USAID will seek to strengthen local governments' outreach and dialogue with the community in order to provide for a clear connection between ordinary citizens and administrative and management personnel at the local government level.

Ensuring gender equality is an important element in achieving more effective responsive local government. USAID programming will ensure that its work with local governments places special emphasis on ensuring equal access to improved services, establishing gender equality in budgeting, and capturing the priorities and needs of both women and men in strategic planning. USAID will work with local governments to identify and address barriers to women's participation in decision making.

Sub-IR 1.3.2 Increased Financial Viability of Public Services
At the same time as USAID supports improved capacity within local governments, it is important that the public services which they provide be financially viable as a means to ensure their sustainability. At the present time, the fees for provision of many basic public services, such as water and energy, are not tied to the actual costs of provision. Local revenues are not sufficient to cover the outstanding costs, and local governments do not have other means to reduce the deficit. Through this sub-IR USAID will help to support activities which will improve the financial viability of service provision at the local level, including improved cost allocation, increased revenue generation through improved billing and collection of fees, and increased efficiency of public services in order to decrease overall cost. Energy efficiency, in particular, will be an area of focus for the improvement of the financial viability of public services, as energy costs represent a major portion of local government expenditure at the same time as energy use at the local level is highly inefficient. Savings in energy costs overall and a reduction in the use of energy by local governments will make an important contribution to local governments' ability to provide for a broader range of basic public services.

Development Objective 2: Increased Investment and Trade in Targeted Sectors

The Moldova Economic Growth Assessment, which informs this strategy, identified a number of "binding constraints" that have a negative impact on Moldova's rate of economic growth. At the center of the Economic Growth assessment's findings is that due to factors including inefficiency, corruption, energy dependency and inefficiency, and a lack of incentives for entrepreneurship, "there is a broad consensus that both markets and firms in Moldova are uncompetitive." As a result of the assessment, assistance needs to address both areas in which Moldova is uncompetitive by improving the economic foundations for growth as well as working to strengthen the private sector. Additionally, barriers to economic empowerment of women in Moldova include time constraints due to heavy household labor responsibilities, active discrimination on the part of employers, stratification of women into lower-paying sectors, and low numbers of women in managerial positions, among others.

This DO responds directly to these challenges, targeting assistance to both priorities in order to allow for the increased levels of economic activity which are necessary to achieve improved living standards. The successful implementation of this DO will help to free Moldova's private sector actors from unnecessary regulation, while at the same time helping the government to identify and promote economic reforms, and stimulate investment, trade, and job growth in sectors with export potential.

The activities under this DO will ultimately lead to economic growth based on strengthening private sector competitiveness through increased trade and investment in strategic sectors, supporting increased job creation and providing more economic opportunities for Moldovans. It will be important to ensure coordination between efforts in the area of energy, including regionally-funded USAID efforts, the work of other donors and the host government, and activities supported by

USAID/Moldova. Regionally-funded efforts such as support for the development of a low emissions development strategy (LEDS) and integration into regional energy markets will leverage USAID/Moldova in-country support to ensure host country participation and coordination. At the same time, USAID/Moldova efforts will increase energy efficiency at the municipal level, seek opportunities to increase access to credit for energy efficiency investment, and support Embassy and intra-donor coordination efforts in the energy area. Successful implementation of this DO will also require careful alignment of resources with other donors and host government priorities and programs. In particular, activities are aligned with investments from the EU, the World Bank, the EBRD and the European Investment Bank (EIB). In the case of investments in economic infrastructure, which is identified as a binding constraint, USAID assistance will focus on enhancing the capacity for sustainable Public Private Partnerships in areas such as water infrastructure and quality standards.

Intermediate Result (IR) 2.1: Improved Economic Foundation for Growth
In order for private sector actors to be able to compete domestically and regionally, Moldova must strengthen its foundation for private sector-led economic growth by offering a business environment that is favorable to entrepreneurship and attractive to investors. The Moldova Economic Growth assessment identified constraints in the areas of access to finance and in the trade enabling environment as the most important limitations in developing this foundation. The assessment also highlighted Moldova's geographic position as being an important factor in determining this growth strategy. The assessment notes that as a "small, landlocked, and resource-poor" country, Moldova must focus on its connections to the region as a primary enabling factor for trade and investment. Moreover, in order to help stem the outflow of migrants seeking economic opportunities abroad - particularly including women and men who are vulnerable to human trafficking, Moldova must offer greater economic opportunities for all citizens. In particular, trade facilitation, increasing regional trade, and improving the business and trade enabling environment should be considered as critical factors in developing Moldova's foundation for broad-based economic growth. The activities under this IR will directly target the need for a strong foundation for economic growth, focusing efforts on creating a "level playing field" for Moldova's private sector and on enabling growth in those economic sectors where Moldova has a competitive advantage. Success in this IR will involve coordinating USAID investments with the work of other donors, particularly the World Bank, the EU, SIDA, the EBRD, the EIB, and the Government of Romania.

Another key element of Moldova's economic foundation for growth is the existence of a functioning justice system capable of protecting the rights of investors and settling disputes in a timely fashion. This area of assistance is addressed under IR 1.2 "Justice System is More Transparent and Accountable." By strengthening justice sector institutions, particularly by including improved judicial capacity, work in this IR will have a direct impact on improving Moldova's foundation for economic growth through providing increased protection of investors against corruption.

Sub-IR 2.1.1 Improved Business and Trade Enabling Environment
This sub-IR will focus on the legal and regulatory systems, the implementation of policies, and public-private dialogue, which provide a framework for private-sector-led growth in Moldova. By identifying

and addressing bottlenecks in the processes through which businesses engage with public sector entities - such as licenses, fees, permits, customs/duties, and tax procedures - activities under this sub-IR will seek to reduce the time and cost to the private sector of complying with these requirements. At the same time, USAID assistance will increase the efficiency of these processes so that the government of Moldova is able to facilitate private sector activity while also being able to gather statistical information and collect appropriate fees. Frequent and collaborative communication between public and private sector actors is also fundamental to establishing an environment in which businesses can flourish. USAID will emphasize the need for regular public-private dialogue through which the private sector can inform and seek to influence government policies. USAID will also help to foster improved public-private dialogue through strengthening industry associations and supporting their capacity to communicate industry needs to policy makers. Successful implementation of this sub-IR will speed up and clarify the processes that govern the private sector and will improve the ability to trade across borders, particularly with the EU.

Adequate "hard" physical infrastructure such as roads, bridges, energy generation/transmission, landfills, and communications equipment, are a fundamental requirement for Moldova's economic growth as a prerequisite for businesses to operate competitively. While U.S. resources available for implementation of this strategy do not provide for substantial investments in such infrastructure, other donors and the host government are engaged in infrastructure development. Successful implementation of this DO assumes that important donor and government-funded investments in transportation, energy, and communications, in particular, continue to move forward. For these investments in critical infrastructure to take place, Public Private Partnerships (PPPs) must play a part. Without investment in such partnerships, the public sector alone will not be able to develop key sectors such as transportation which are critical to broad-based economic development. USAID will work with other donors and the Moldovan government to facilitate improvements in physical infrastructure by focusing assistance on the legal, regulatory and policy requirements for infrastructure development, and in particular those necessary to strengthen the enabling environment for the development of new PPPs. In addition, USAID will collaborate with the MCC through the course of implementation of the MCC Compact, which includes transportation and irrigation infrastructure components.

USAID will also focus attention on developing local capacity on "soft" infrastructure such as quality, certifications, and accreditations, in order to meet international standards required for exports by businesses in Moldova's most competitive economic sectors. Moldova's integration into the EU economy, as well as its ability to seek new international markets and strengthen export-led growth, requires that technical barriers to trade of this type be functional and credible. These systems, known as quality infrastructure, define Moldova's ability to trade effectively - in particular as Moldova finalizes a comprehensive free trade agreement with the EU and expands its access to the EU market. Specifically, the term "quality infrastructure" refers to systems of measurement, standardization, testing, and quality management, certification and accreditation (abbreviated as MSTQ) and comprises efforts to eliminate non-customs and non-tariff related trade barriers through improvements to these systems. USAID will provide assistance under this sub-IR to develop such quality infrastructure specifically to promote increased trade. Support to key MSTQ requirements such as phyto-sanitary agricultural controls, for example, will enable agricultural producers to meet strict certification requirements for agricultural exports. Assistance will also focus on bringing together the public and private sectors to foster partnerships that have the potential to enhance institutional sustainability. USAID will ensure appropriate gender balance for task forces and training activities is achieved when developing approaches to improve the business enabling environment.

Sub-IR 2.1.2 Increased Access to Finance

As noted in the October 2012 Moldova High Level Financial Sector Overview[9], "The small size of the financial sector and the limited range of financial services continue to hold back economic growth in the Moldovan private sector." While banks in Moldova are well-capitalized, the Economic Growth assessment also noted that in many cases banks are either unwilling to lend due to an incomplete understanding of risk, or do not lend because of a mismatch between the bank's credit products and terms and the requirements of potential borrowers. The availability of appropriate credit instruments and terms is a basic requirement in Moldova given the country's trade-based approach to sustain economic growth. At the same time, there is very low public confidence in the banking system, with corresponding low savings rates. USAID assistance will focus on the development of appropriate credit guarantee instruments that will encourage banks to extend credit to new borrowers based on a better understanding and reduction of the bank's exposure to risk. Developing an approach to increase the low savings rates, which could include leveraging regionally-funded investments that will work on improvements to deposit insurance schemes, will help to improve public confidence in the banking sector. New credit guarantees will focus on economic sectors that have a competitive advantage for domestic and regional trade; and that do not have access to affordable, appropriate credit instruments such as energy efficiency. Opportunities to increase access to credit among women and other vulnerable groups will be actively sought. To alleviate the energy issues, USAID will also explore utilizing Development Credit Authority funds for lending to MSMEs to promote energy efficiency and renewable energy. USAID assistance in this area will complement larger investments from the EU, the World Bank and the EIB in capitalizing loan facilities for key economic sectors.

IR 2.2: Improved Private Sector Competitiveness in Selected Industries

Many enterprises in Moldova lack strategic vision and customer focus, follow inefficient internal business processes, and lag behind regional competitors in adopting new technology to increase productivity and competitiveness. To achieve a growing export-led economy, Moldova needs to find solutions to these persistent problems and innovate within traditional industries. In addition, Moldova must move beyond its traditional economic sectors and develop new competitive sectors. To encourage these changes, entrepreneurs need to have the freedom to innovate and have access to support from institutions that nurture new business development. At the same time, there is an increasing demand for management information systems and process improvement procedures and systems.

---

[9] October 2012 Prepared by the Partners for Financial Stability Program, Deloitte Consulting LLC for USAID.

Businesses are the engine for economic growth in Moldova and increasing the competitiveness of key industries represents the most direct way to stimulate increased trade and investment. In a 2009 USAID study, for example, the author describes the goal of such competitiveness interventions: "When successful, competitiveness projects result in increased business investment; increased sales, revenue and employment; business expansion; increased productivity and higher wages; and consequently, improved standards of living." As such, support to this sub-IR directly supports achievement of the DO as well as the overall CDCS goal. Successful implementation of the IR will require that USAID contribute to increased productivity and expanded market linkages for high-value exports. In addition, USAID will increase the availability of skilled men and women, trained workers through partnerships with industries as well as through linkages to the host government and universities.

USAID will develop strategies to ensure that inputs from women owned and operated businesses within each targeted sector are included in the enterprise development process and identify leading female entrepreneurs and business-owners who will serve as role models for other women in business. USAID will also seek opportunities to expand economic growth activities in Transnistria, including support for MSME development, with assistance focused on, but not limited to, agricultural MSMEs. The level of engagement in Transnistria will depend on the level of access and security arrangements that can be arranged with Transnistrian representatives. Currently, activities are promoting person-to-person linkages and trust building across both banks by carrying out agriculture training events in Transnistria and by including Transnistrian high-value agriculture farmers in study tours with other Moldovans. Assistance also includes activities to enhance the capacity of Transnistrian business service providers to support MSMEs in the areas of business management, quality and productivity.

Sub-IR 2.2.1 Increased Productivity
USAID assistance will help targeted industries[10] in Moldova to become more productive through efforts to streamline business processes and to incorporate modern equipment and technology into the production cycle. This assistance will include international expert consultants in selected industries in order to help Moldovan companies adapt to regional markets. Overall, a lack of business sophistication is one of the root causes of low productivity in Moldovan businesses. This can be addressed by seeking opportunities for mentoring and twinning visits to provide cost-effective ways for Moldovan businesses to improve business operations and strategies. In addition, by helping to build and expand the influence of industry associations, USAID will also help to consolidate industries around core competitiveness strategies and help them to identify areas where working together is more productive than remaining disconnected. In the area of agriculture, for example, USAID will support the development of high-value agricultural production as a leading national export. Women in agriculture networks will also be fostered in the regions to provide a forum for training sessions and exchanges to advocate for agribusiness issues of particular relevance to women producer groups. Activities will be aimed at

---

[10]The currently-identified sectors include high-value agriculture, wine, IT, apparel and footwear, furniture, and tourism. These sectors are being constantly evaluated along with other emerging sectors, so the focus may adapt through the life of the CDCS.

developing leadership skills and enabling networking among women farmers and agribusiness operators.

Success in this approach will require that actors across the value chain, from producers to consolidators, transporters, business service providers, and ultimately exporters, work together for their mutual benefit. No individual enterprise in this industry or any other in Moldova is large enough to alone make Moldova competitive in the international market. By linking enterprises through industry associations and other industry-level outreach, however, USAID can help to raise the productivity and quality of targeted sectors as well as help to build enough scale to attract increased investment and buyer interest. At the firm level, USAID will also work directly with targeted enterprises in order to improve their productivity, particularly in the case where there is not yet an industry association which has emerged to support industry-wide development. To paraphrase Dr. Michael Porter, a leading authority on competitiveness, industries are not competitive, companies are. In this sense, it is critical that USAID also seek to identify key enterprises in Moldova that have the capacity to act as industry leaders and provide targeted assistance to improve their productivity as a means to support sector-wide growth. USAID will also seek opportunities to target assistance to women-owned enterprises to support more gender-equitable opportunities and growth within the targeted sectors.

As educated, skilled people migrate from Moldova seeking jobs, they take with them the most basic resource that businesses need in order to compete: a high-quality workforce. This was highlighted by the Economic Growth assessment team as a widespread lack of qualified workers to meet demand across all key industries. Labor force weaknesses are now increasingly acknowledged as a major impediment to growth in Moldova, and the American Chamber of Commerce in Moldova recommends that developing the workforce should be one of four national priorities for Moldova. The Moldovan government's primary development strategy document, Moldova 2020, also stresses the importance of developing Moldova's human capital. In support of enhancing productivity, USAID will work with the private sector to help increase and retain adequate skilled workers through developing industry-specific training and job certification plans, which are connected with employment opportunities, as well as working with government to help address the need for up-to-date training in key technical areas. Implementation will involve coordination with other donors, particularly the EU, which are focusing resources on skills development and vocational/technical training. Human and institutional capacity development initiatives such as these will help to build the workforce which the private sector needs to compete domestically and regionally.

Sub-IR 2.2.2 Expanded Market Linkages

Moldova must expand its efforts to provide incentives for companies to increase their linkages with regional markets in order to increase trade and investment into productive economic sectors. USAID efforts under this sub-IR will complement ongoing donor and government efforts to strengthen the Moldovan import-export promotion agency, including strengthening linkages between the Moldovan diaspora and investment opportunities in Moldova. Working through industry associations, USAID will assist targeted sectors to develop specific recommendations for policy makers regarding the critical needs for industries to increase exports. Through policy and regulatory improvements, USAID will work with the Government of Moldova to increase incentives for companies to expand exports, while at the same time helping to increase enterprises' access to business support services. In addition, USAID will work to help develop branding information for Moldovan industries in targeted sectors, allowing industry associations and individual enterprises to market themselves more effectively in the regional European and CIS markets.

Critical Assumptions and Risks

Achieving the Mission's Development Objectives depends on several critical assumptions and the mitigation of certain risks. The critical assumptions are as follows:

(1) The Government of Moldova, be it the AIE or another party or coalition, remains committed to adopting economic and democratic reforms.
(2) The economies of the Eurozone and European countries at-large do not deteriorate back to crisis levels.
(3) Interaction with Transnistria remains at status-quo or gradually progresses towards greater integration.
(4) Key donor partners, including the EU and World Bank, continue their assistance to Moldova at comparable levels.

IV. Monitoring, Evaluation and Learning

Monitoring - Illustrative performance indicators for the Results Framework Goal, Development Objectives (DOs), Intermediate Results (IRs), and Sub-IRs are shown in Annex 2. In line with the guidance, the Mission will develop a new Performance Management Plan (PMP) within four months of CDCS approval. The PMP will enable the Mission to monitor and manage a core set of performance indicators that reflect appropriate targets, baselines, and data collection and analysis approaches. Project-level Performance Monitoring and Evaluation Plans (PMEP) will also be reviewed to ensure alignment with the new PMP and adjusted as appropriate.

Evaluation - Illustrative evaluation questions for each DO are shown in Annex 2. Performance evaluations on all "large projects" will be conducted over the course of the CDCS period to examine whether interventions are achieving the intended results in the Results Framework and provide lessons-learned to inform future project designs. While USAID has not identified opportunities for an impact evaluation, the joint USAID/MCC Agriculture Competitiveness and Enterprise Development project will be conducting an MCC-lead impact evaluation.

Learning - With all of the Mission's current large projects ending within the strategy period, the Mission will be guided by a continuous learning approach to inform project design and prioritization, taking into account considerations such as the evolving sectorial context and needs, other donor activities, USAID Forward objectives, and progress and lessons-learned from current projects.

Annex 1 - Abbreviations and Acronyms

AIE	Alliance for European Integration
CDCS	Country Development Cooperation Strategy
CIS	Commonwealth of Independent States
CSO	Civil Society Organization
DO	Development Objective
DRG	Democracy, Human Rights, and Governance
EBRD	European Bank for Reconstruction and Development
EIB	European Investment Bank
EU	European Union
GDP	Gross Domestic Product
GOM	Government of the Republic of Moldova
IMF	International Monetary Fund
INL	State Department's Bureau of International Narcotics and Law Enforcement
IOM	International Organization for Migration
IR	Intermediate Result
JRS	Joint Regional Strategy
MCC	Millennium Challenge Corporation
MCP	Monitoring Country Progress Analysis
MSME	Micro, small and medium enterprise
MSSR	Moldovan Soviet Socialist Republic
MSTQ	Measurement, standardization, testing, and quality management, certification and accreditation
NSD	National Strategy for Decentralization
OSCE	Organization for Security and Cooperation in Europe
PCRM	Communist Party of the Republic of Moldova
PPP	Public Private Partnership
SIDA	Swedish International Development Agency
UN	United Nations
UNDP	United Nations Development Program
USAID	United States Agency for International Development
WEF	World Economic Forum

Annex 2 - Illustrative Performance Indicators and Evaluation Questions

Goal: A Better-Governed Moldova with Improved Living Standards for its Citizens

1. World Bank – Worldwide Governance Indicators: Voice and Accountability, and Government Effectiveness
2. UNDP – International Human Development Index (Living Standards Dimension): GNI per capita (PPP$)

DO1: More Effective and Accountable Democratic Governance

1. Freedom House - Nations in Transit Indicators: Civil Society; Judicial Framework and Independence; and Local Democratic Governance

Evaluation Questions:

1. To what extent are CSOs better able to advocate for citizens and their needs? How are citizens more engaged in decision-making at the three levels of government -- either directly or through CSO intermediaries? How has government responsiveness to citizens' needs changed in localities that received US assistance? What are the major factors that contributed to this change?

2. To what extent are the benefits of local government interventions expected to be sustainable? What were the major factors that influenced the sustainability of the interventions? Are the interventions more sustainable in areas where a complementary G2G mechanism was implemented? What other major differences were observed in localities that received additional assistance through the G2G mechanism?

Intermediate Result (IR) 1.1: Increased Citizen Engagement in Governmental Decision-Making

1. Number of new mechanisms established for providing civil society input into governmental decision-making
2. USAID CSO Sustainability Index: Advocacy and Infrastructure

Sub IR 1.1.1 More Effective and Sustainable Civil Society

1. Number of policy changes, regulations, and procedures adopted by GOM with CSO input
2. Number of watchdog activities implemented by CSOs receiving US assistance
3. USAID CSO Sustainability Index: Organizational Capacity

Sub-IR 1.1.2 More Inclusive and Representative Political Participation

1. Number of formal and informal civil society groups engaging with political parties to promote issues critical to constituents
2. Number of local council factions engaged in recurring dialogue with constituencies
3. Number of meetings between party policy-working-groups and party subgroups on policy issues (including the women chapter)

IR 1.2: Justice System is More Transparent and Accountable

1. Number of Moldovan courts that fully use the integrated case management and the audio-recording systems

2. Number of approved and implemented laws/regulations that ensure a better functioning of the judiciary (regulations referring to courts management, functioning of the judicial body, etc.)

Sub-IR 1.2.1 Increased Citizen Demand for Effective Justice

1. Percentage increase of court users/litigant's satisfaction level with the justice sector - court user/citizen assessment and satisfaction with court services including access to the courts, fairness and integrity, timeliness and expedition, and their general trust and confidence in the court.

2. Number of citizens reached through public legal information campaigns (disaggregated by sex)

Sub-IR 1.2.2 More Capable and Professional Justice System

1. Number of justice sector personnel trained (disaggregated by sex)

2. Ratio of case dispositions to case filings (number of judgments and other decisions confirmed in relation to a total number of complaints considered)

3. Number of quality improvements implemented by the National Institute of Justice (curricula, management, training methodologies and evaluation of skills process)

IR 1.3: Strengthened Local Government Capacity

1. Percentage of sub-national government institutions receiving US assistance that improve performance

Sub-IR 1.3.1 Improved Management Systems and More Participatory Processes

1. Percentage of local governments applying improved mechanisms of transparency and accountability towards citizens

2. Percentage of the population indicating qualitative improvements in the assisted processes and/or systems (disaggregated by sex)

3. Number of integrated service-improvement-plans completed by local governments

Sub-IR 1.3.2 Increased Financial Viability of Public Services

1. Percent increase in revenues of towns receiving US assistance

2. Number of municipalities increasing revenues collected from property tax

3. Number of defined services that achieve improved cost recovery

DO2: Increased Investment and Trade in Targeted Sectors

1. Percentage change in trade volume in targeted sectors

2. Value of new private sector investment in targeted sectors

Evaluation Questions:

1. To what extent have improvements in the business-enabling environment (BEE) contributed to increased investments and trade?

2. Which BEE areas of interventions were most cost-effective in advancing the development objective? *BEE areas are defined by the topic areas in the WB Doing Business Survey.

Intermediate Result (IR) 2.1: Improved Economic Foundation for Growth

1. Change in World Bank - Ease of Doing Business Survey: Paying Taxes, Investor Protection, Access to Credit, Trading Across Borders
2. Change in percent of key stakeholders in the private sector who express positive opinion of the effort to reform the business enabling environment

Sub-IR 2.1.1 Improved Business and Trade Enabling Environment

1. Number of times government has adopted or revised laws, rules, or regulations with advocacy support by private sector associations through transparent processes to benefit the general business environment
2. Number of US-assisted entities providing international standards certification
3. Number of US-assisted private sector or public-private partnerships related to infrastructure (energy, ICT, roads, etc.)

Sub-IR 2.1.2 Increased Access to Finance

1. Value of loans disbursed to the private sector from financial institutions receiving US assistance
2. Outstanding domestic credit to the private sector as a percentage of GDP
3. Proportion of female participants in U.S. government-assisted programs designed to increase access to productive economic resources (assets, credit, income or employment)

IR 2.2: Improved Private Sector Competitiveness in Selected Industries

1. World Economic Forum (WEF) – Global Competitiveness Index: Goods Market Efficiency
2. Dollar value of increase in sales in industries funded by US assistance

Sub-IR 2.2.1 Increased Productivity

1. WEF Technological Readiness Index
2. WEF Business Sophistication Index
3. Percentage change in specified productivity measure (sales/inputs)

Sub-IR 2.2.2 Expanded Market Linkages

1. Number of innovative trade breakthroughs: new markets, products, etc.
2. Change in dollar value of exports to non-traditional/new markets in targeted sectors

Annex 3 - Highlights of Moldova's Monitoring Country Progress Gap Analysis
June 2012

Overview. Moldova lags well behind the 11 E&E graduate countries on all five MCP dimensions, though most notably in democratic reforms and human capital. By Eurasian standards, however, Moldova's economic and democratic reform profile is among the more advanced, alongside Georgia and Ukraine.

Economic reforms. Moldova is more advanced in first stage macroeconomic reforms compared to the seven E&E Eurasian countries on average, though it is E&E Eurasian average in second stage macroeconomic reforms. As with most of the E&E Eurasian countries, macroeconomic reforms in Moldova have stagnated in recent years. In contrast, Moldova has made notable gains in business environment (or microeconomic) reforms in recent years, though the gains have not been linear. From the World Bank's *Doing Business* dataset, the most significant business environment constraints in Moldova have been dealing with construction permits, getting electricity, and trading across borders.

Democratic reforms. As with E&E Eurasia overall, democratic reforms in Moldova have regressed on balance since at least 1996 (the first year of Freedom House's *Nations in Transit* dataset). Of the seven democratization areas measured, civil society is the most advanced in Moldova, and it is the only aspect that has advanced on balance since 1996. Moldova's independent media has made notable gains in 2010 and 2011, though there was considerable backsliding in earlier years, from 1996 to 2009. Public governance has regressed the most from 1996 to 2011 in Moldova. In both the non-governmental organization and media sectors, the greatest challenges seem to stem from economic pressures.

Macroeconomic performance. Annual economic growth has been high for most years since at least 2004 to the present; the salient exception is the six percent contraction of GDP in 2009, in the depths of the global economic crisis. The longer term economic output picture for Moldova is more sobering. The economies of Moldova and Ukraine were the last economies in the E&E region to resume positive economic growth after the transition depressions, not until the year 2000. The economies of Moldova, Ukraine, and Georgia remain well below their respective sizes prior to the collapse of communism. The size of the export sector relative to GDP in Moldova is relatively small and has been declining since the mid-1990s. Imports have far outweighed exports in Moldova's economy, contributing to chronically high current account deficits. Labor productivity is the lowest in the E&E region. Remittances are very substantial; close to one-fourth of the total active population in Moldova has been working abroad. Notwithstanding recent progress in energy sector reforms, Moldova has one of the most energy inefficient economies worldwide and one of the more energy dependent ones as well.

Human capital. Moldova's human capital has both extremes; very low (poor) scores on per capita income, life expectancy, and the incidences of tuberculosis, while very high scores in public expenditures in health and education. Life expectancy in Moldova in 2010 was 69 years, an increase from 67 years in 2000. Of the 7 E&E Eurasia countries, only Russia has a life expectancy as low as Moldova's. Infectious disease trends are troubling. The tuberculosis incidence in Moldova has been steadily increasing since 1997 and is among the highest in the E&E region. The HIV incidence rate in 2009 is significantly higher than what it was in 2000.

Moldova lags behind E&E standards in primary school enrollment, and with a trend of declining enrollment since the mid-2000s. Upper secondary enrollment rates in Moldova are well below E&E standards overall. While steadily increasing, such rates in Moldova remain less than 60%. This is slightly higher than enrollments rates in the Central Asian Republics. Functional literacy test results for Moldovan students show results below OECD standards, though not alarmingly so. According to the IMF, a large proportion of public spending on education is wasted in maintaining empty schools and small classes.

Peace and Security. Moldova ranks 18th out of 29 E&E countries in MCP's peace and security index. Of the six peace and security areas, Moldova lags considerably and lags the most in its capacity to combat weapons of mass destruction, with low scores in export control of chemical and biological weapons.

Annex 4 - Key Findings of USAID Gender Assessment

March 2011

- There was relative consensus across informants that the most pressing gender issues in Moldova include women's economic empowerment, the high incidence of domestic violence (DV), the interconnected issues of migration and trafficking in persons (TIP), and the low level of female representation in political parties and elected office.

- Although Moldova is not an oppressively patriarchal culture, there are still relatively strong gender roles and women are generally expected to have primary responsibility for the household and for child care whether they are employed or not, thus creating the familiar "double burden" of work in and outside of the home.

- Many Moldovans are familiar with the term "gender", however, the differences between "sex" and "gender" are not well-understood. Most Moldovans, including government officials are said to assume that "gender" refers exclusively to women and concerns about "women's issues".

- There appears to be reluctance in Moldovan society to accept gender equality as an important concept, and men are particularly likely not to see the benefits of empowering women and promoting equal opportunities.

- Current legislation along with various provisions in more specialized laws and legal codes are considered to represent a solid basis for gender equality and lack of discrimination in Moldova. Nevertheless, there are serious barriers that prevent these laws from realizing the desired impact, including the slow pace of concrete implementation, inadequacy of budgetary resources, and associated reliance on donor funding.

- In carrying out its work, the Government of Moldova (and others) suffer from a lack of sex-disaggregated statistics in many areas. A survey of relevant stakeholders carried out by United Nations Development Fund for Women revealed that there is a strong demand for sex-disaggregated data, that government workers need additional training on the value and use of such statistics, and that users desire analysis of the data in addition to tables and charts.

- The Department for Equal Opportunities and the Prevention of Violence in the Ministry of Labor, Social Protection and Family appears to have the will to carry out its responsibilities to oversee the implementation of the National Action Plan on Gender but is under-staffed and under-resourced. Focal points for addressing gender equality in line Ministries and at the local level are not yet functioning effectively.

- The current Government is collaborating well with civil society on issues related to gender equality and gender-based violence.

- There is a small group of active "women's NGOs" that are high in capacity and consistently active in addressing gender issues but they struggle with sustainability and are almost completely dependent on donor funding.

- While not blatantly discriminatory, the media conveys different messages about men and women, including that women are less likely to be experts or thought-leaders.

- Women are under-represented at all levels of government in Moldova and there is current discussion of beefing up electoral code provisions that would require political parties to reserve 30% of the slots on candidate lists for women.
- Domestic violence is a serious problem in Moldova and there are not yet sufficient services for assisting victims of violence or for treating male perpetrators.
- Trafficking in persons (TIP) continues to be a pressing problem for Moldova and the patterns of TIP appear to be changing with traffickers becoming more sophisticated and nuanced in their methods, levels of internal trafficking beginning to rise, more male victims of trafficking being identified, and according to some, children becoming increasingly vulnerable to sex tourists.
- Migration of parents out of Moldova has been identified as leading to negative psychological outcomes for their children who remain behind, raising fears that a generation of children and youth will grow up without the benefits of parental supervision and in-person care, and with distorted perceptions of gender roles in family life.
- Large numbers of women and men are inactive in the labor market in Moldova and somewhat more men than women are registered as unemployed.
- Women are much less likely than men to be business owners and the female entrepreneurs that do exist are concentrated in the micro-business sector.
- Barriers to economic empowerment of women in Moldova include time constraints due to heavy responsibilities for household labor, active discrimination on the part of employers, stratification of women into lower-paying sectors, and low numbers of women in managerial positions, among others.

Annex 5 - Summary of Donor Mapping Report
September 2012

1.1 Main Development Partners` Strategies

The strategies of the most important development partners of Moldova are an efficient instrument of understanding the priorities which animate the activities of these institutions and countries. The main three development partners of the Republic of Moldova are the European Union, the World Bank, and the United Nations. Several other important development partners like Sweden, the European Bank for Reconstruction and Development, Austria have been introduced in this development partners profile list for a more elaborate analysis.

The strategies used for mapping development partners' plans for aiding Moldova end mostly in 2012-2014. For example, the World Bank strategy was conceived for a four-year period, ending in 2012, European Union's NIP is lasting until 2013 and Sweden Strategy for Development Cooperation with the Republic of Moldova will end in 2014. In fact, the major development partners will feel very soon the necessity to write new strategies after examining the results of the current ones.

Strategy Documents used for mapping external donors' activities in the Republic of Moldova

Donor	Strategy document	Website
EU	NIP-2010-2013	http://ec.europa.eu/world/enp/pdf/country/2011_enp_nip_moldova_en.pdf
World Bank	CSP 2009-2012	http://documents.worldbank.org/curated/en/2010/12/13230709/moldova-country-partnership-strategy-2009-2012
EBRD	EBRD Strategy for Moldova 2010 - 2013	http://www.ebrd.com/downloads/country/strategy/moldova.pdf
Romania	Romania supported countries	http://www.euroresources.org/guide/donor_profiles/ro_romania.html
EIB	Factsheet EIB financing in the EU's Eastern Neighbors	http://www.eib.org/infocentre/publications/all/eib_factsheet_central_eastern_europe.htm

ONE-UN	Moldova UNDAF 2013-2017 ONE UNITED NATIONS PARTNERSHIP FRAMEWORK 2013 – 2017	http://www.un.md/news_room/pr/2012/undaf/United_Nations_Republic_of_Moldova_Partnership_Framework.pdf
Sweden (SIDA)	Strategy for development cooperation with the Republic of Moldova January 2011 – December 2014	http://www.regeringen.se/sb/d/108/a/32910
Swiss (SDC)	Swiss Cooperation Strategy 2010-2013 Special Program Republic of Moldova	http://www.swiss-cooperation.admin.ch/moldova/en/Home/Swiss_cooperation_with_Moldova/Strategy_and_Objectives
Germany (GIZ, IRZ KfW)	GIZ priorities for MD IRZ-030812 German Financial Cooperation with the RM – the profile of KfW	http://www.kfw-entwicklungsbank.de/ebank/EN_Home/Countries_and_Programmes/Europe/Moldova/KfW_in_Moldova_at_a_Glance.pdf
China	Moldova and the Chinese economic expansion (article OSW Commentary)	http://www.osw.waw.pl/en/publikacje/osw-commentary/2012-05-28/ukraine-belarus-and-moldova-and-chinese-economic-expansion-east
Austria (ADA)	Moldova Country Strategy 2010–2015	http://www.entwicklung.at/uploads/media/CS_Moldova_2011-2015.pdf

1.2 Mapping of Development Partners' Activities

The most important development partners who assumed the task to contribute substantially to the development of the Republic of Moldova as part of Rethink Moldova are listed in Figure 1. They were catalogued according to five areas: 1) Democracy, Human Rights and Governance; 2) Health, Education and Social Protection and Services; 3) Economic Growth and Trade; 4) Conflict Mitigation and reconciliation; and 5) Humanitarian Assistance. The figure shows that donors are most prone to invest in the economic growth and trade area, which includes such projects as infrastructure and agriculture. The second most attractive area for external donors is Democracy, Human Rights and Governance, which includes work with civil society, the justice sector and central and local authorities. These two areas match the GOM's stated priorities.

www.ingramcontent.com/pod-product-compliance
Lightning Source LLC
Chambersburg PA
CBHW080637290526
45790CB00007B/3107